Published By Adam Gilbin

@ Jeff Adler

Time Management: A Self Help Stress

Management Guide to Goal Setting, Improving

Productivity Habits and Focus

All Right RESERVED

ISBN 978-87-94477-64-2

TABLE OF CONTENTS

Chapter 1 1

The Power Of Being Conscious And Focused 1

Chapter 2 6

Mind-Body Connection: Holistic Approaches To Stress Reduction 6

Chapter 3 14

Getting Started 14

Chapter 4 19

Introduction To Planning With Perspective: Building Effective Time Strategies 19

Chapter 5 24

Loving And Respecting Others Overview 24

Chapter 6 57

Assessing Your Current Time Usage 57

Chapter 7 65

Creating Your Personalized Time Management System 65

Chapter 8 75

Understanding Prioritization Techniques 75

Chapter 1

The Power of Being Conscious and Focused

Practicing Mindfulness to Enhance Concentration

Mindfulness means being active, present, and conscious of your thoughts and feelings. Adapting consciousness into your routine improves your ability to focus on the present. Here, we'll explore mindfulness exercises that can sharpen your awareness and attention.

Activity: Mindful Breathing Exercise

Engage in a simple mindful breathing exercise. Relax in a quiet place, and focus your attention on breathing in and out. Take note of each inhale and exhale as you breathe. If your attention begins to wander, focus your attention back on breathing. Regular practice of this exercise can enhance your ability to concentrate.

Overcoming Procrastination through Mindful Techniques

Procrastination is a drawback to effective time management. Procrastination can cause you to lose a great opportunity. Self-awareness helps you understand the causes of procrastination and ways to overcome it. Cultivate self-awareness and compassion, to address the factors contributing to procrastination. Replace avoidance behaviors with proactive, mindful action. Be consistent and active in working towards achieving your goals.

Exercise: Procrastination Journal

Keep a journal to document instances of procrastination. Note the triggers, emotions, and thoughts associated with your procrastination episodes. Identify patterns and develop mindful strategies to counteract procrastination tendencies. There are different ways one can procrastinate, take time to understand your triggers.

Techniques to Improve Focus and Reduce Distractions

There are many distractions in our modern lives that pull our attention away from tasks. In this section, we'll explore practical techniques to reduce distractions and maintain focus. Learn to have time for everything. Distractions could be friends, colleagues, or family looking to spend time with you. Whether managing digital distractions or finding a good workspace, these strategies will work. These strategies will empower you to reclaim focus, boost productivity, and set boundaries.

Case Study: Focusing in the Digital Age

Ever wondered how some individuals seem to maintain focus more than others? Find out the strategies they employed to maintain focus despite digital distractions. Learn from their techniques and apply them to yours to enhance your concentration.

Summary

The power of mindfulness and focus is a powerful tool in effective time management. By incorporating mindful practices into your routine you can cultivate a focused mind. Also, put in place techniques to overcome procrastination and cut distractions. A determined mind is not swayed by external interruptions. Immerse yourself in your tasks and make significant steps toward your goals.

In Chapter 5: Effective Planning and Time Blocking, we will explore the art of planning. Also, we will talk about assigning specific time slots for tasks. Through strategic planning and time blocking, you can optimize your productivity. You can also ensure that all tasks get the attention they deserve.

Chapter 2

Mind-Body Connection: Holistic Approaches to Stress Reduction

Welcome to the rejuvenating oasis that is Chapter 4 of our stress-busting journey: the Mind-Body Connection. Today, we're diving into the realm of holistic approaches to stress reduction, where the mind and body waltz together in a symphony of tranquility. So, grab your metaphorical yoga mat and let's explore the blissful world where stress takes a backseat.

Mind and Body: The Dynamic Duo

Picture your mind and body as the dynamic duo, partners in crime against stress. When one feels the pressure, the other lends a helping hand. It's a beautiful dance, and understanding this connection is key to unlocking a realm of stress-relief possibilities.

In this chapter, we'll explore practices that bridge the gap between mind and body, creating a harmonious symphony that sings the sweet melody of stress reduction. From meditation to yoga, these practices aren't just about the physical or mental—they're about the delicious dance where the two intertwine.

Meditation: A Mindful Pause in the Chaos

Let's start with the rockstar of the mindfulness world: meditation. Close your eyes, take a deep breath, and imagine a serene garden where stress is nothing but a passing breeze. That's the magic of meditation—a practice that allows you to hit the pause button on life's chaos.

We'll explore different meditation techniques, from guided visualizations to mindfulness meditation. It's like giving your mind a mini-vacation, allowing it to recharge and return with newfound clarity. Say goodbye to the mental clutter; meditation is your ticket to a stress-free mind.

Yoga: Where Breath Meets Movement

Now, let's roll out the yoga mat and stretch our way to stress relief. Yoga isn't just about striking Instagram-worthy poses (although, that's a bonus); it's about the marriage of breath and movement, creating a dance that nourishes both body and mind.

We'll delve into the world of yoga for stress reduction, exploring beginner-friendly poses and flows. Whether you're a seasoned yogi or a first-time downward dog explorer, there's a yoga practice waiting for you. It's not about contorting your body into a pretzel; it's about finding the sweet spot where breath meets movement, and stress takes a backseat.

Mindfulness in Motion: Walking Meditation and Tai Chi

Not a fan of sitting still? No worries! We've got mindfulness in motion coming your way. From walking meditation to the graceful flow of Tai Chi, these practices allow you to embrace mindfulness while in motion.

Imagine strolling through a peaceful garden, each step a deliberate act of presence. That's the essence of walking meditation—a practice we'll explore together. And for those intrigued by the slow, flowing movements of Tai Chi, get ready to embark on a journey of grace and balance. It's like a moving meditation that brings serenity to both body and mind.

Breathwork: The Rhythmic Symphony of Inhales and Exhales

Now, let's talk about something we all do but rarely pay attention to: breathing. Yes, you heard it right—breathwork is a powerful tool in the stress-busting arsenal. The way you breathe directly influences your stress response, and we're about to unlock the rhythmic symphony of inhales and exhales.

We'll explore different breathwork techniques, from deep belly breathing to the energizing breath of fire. It's like giving your body a reset button, calming the nervous system and inviting relaxation. Breathwork is your secret weapon, ready to be unleashed whenever stress comes knocking.

Holistic Lifestyle Practices: Beyond the Mat

But our journey doesn't end with mats and poses. Holistic approaches to stress reduction extend beyond the yoga studio and meditation cushion. In this section, we'll explore lifestyle practices that contribute to a holistic sense of well-being.

From connecting with nature to practicing gratitude, these lifestyle tweaks are like daily vitamins for your stress resilience. It's not about overhauling your entire life; it's about embracing small, meaningful changes that ripple through your daily experience, creating a tapestry of well-being.

Real-Life Stories: Mind-Body Mastery in Action

To add a sprinkle of inspiration to our exploration, we'll dive into real-life stories of individuals who have mastered the art of mind-body connection for stress reduction. From busy professionals finding solace in meditation to individuals transforming their lives through yoga, these stories showcase the transformative power of holistic approaches.

By learning from those who have walked the path, you'll gain insights and practical tips to infuse mind-body practices into your own stress-busting routine. It's like having a friendly guide who's been there and is passing down the wisdom to help you on your journey.

Conclusion: Embracing the Mind-Body Symphony

And there you have it, stress-soothers! We've explored the mind-body connection and the holistic approaches that create a symphony of stress reduction. Whether you're a meditation maestro, a yoga enthusiast, or a breathwork beginner, there's a practice waiting for you.

In the chapters ahead, we'll continue our stress-busting adventure, exploring resilience-building strategies, time management, and the intricate dance of relationships. So, keep that positive energy flowing, and get ready for more friendly guidance, practical tips, and a touch of humor as we journey toward a life with less stress and more joy. The mind-body symphony is playing—let's dance!

CHAPTER 3

Getting started

In this chapter we will show you how to get started and begin changing the way you do things. You'll need to think about what you want to change and why. What are the paybacks you are looking to achieve and how do you motivate yourself to get started?

We'll also reveal the greatest source of your time management problems. This might just surprise you. Finally, we need to think about what you can and can't control. Time management can help to deal with stress, but it can't stop things happening that are outside our control.

WHAT PREVENTS US FROM CHANGING THINGS?

So what is it that prevents us from changing? We all know that we should change various aspects of our lives, but often we never get around to making the first move. All change involves an element of risk. There are four main reasons why we don't change things:

Fear of failure

Fear of success

The enormity of the task

Other people

Fear of failure

We worry that we are not going to succeed and that prevents us from trying in the first place. This can be based on previous negative experiences.

Fear of success

Sometimes it is easier to leave things as they are. We prefer to stay in our comfort zone.

The enormity of the task

Sometimes the enormity of a task makes us think it is best left undone. We look at all the time and effort needed to complete the task and give up. The key is to break big tasks down into smaller tasks and begin working on them. Keep in mind: 'How do you eat an elephant? One mouthful at a time!'

Other people

Other people can influence our self-esteem and confidence. It is very important to develop a positive self-image so that you have the confidence to change things. The view we have of ourselves is often developed in childhood by those people who most influence our behaviour and our lives.

SO HOW DO WE GET STARTED?

Let's start by looking at you. You may have a job or a career, you may have a family and friends, or you may just have friends. If you look at everyone's life and circumstances they are all different, so I am not assuming that everyone reading this book has a wife/ husband, kids, a job, a mortgage and plays golf. What this chapter will do is give some broad principles that anyone can adapt to suit their lifestyle.

A lot of the time when I work with companies as a consultant, they want to make things change. The process I use is to find the answers to four questions:

- Where are you now?
- Where would you like to get to?
- How are you going to get there?
- What's in it for you if it works?

Chapter 4

Introduction to Planning with Perspective: Building Effective Time Strategies

Introduction

In today's fast-paced and demanding world, effective time management has become crucial for individuals and organizations alike. People often find themselves overwhelmed with tasks and responsibilities, struggling to meet deadlines, and feeling a constant sense of urgency. This chapter serves as an introduction to the concept of planning with perspective, which offers a comprehensive approach to building effective time strategies.

2.2 Understanding the Importance of Time Management

Time is an invaluable resource, and managing it efficiently is essential for achieving personal and professional success. Effective time management allows individuals to prioritize tasks, make informed decisions, and allocate adequate time to each activity. By using a perspective-oriented approach, individuals can gain a holistic understanding of their goals, values, and priorities, ultimately leading to better time management.

2.3 Defining Planning with Perspective

Planning with perspective involves taking a step back and evaluating the bigger picture before diving into daily tasks and schedules. It emphasizes aligning actions with long-term goals, creating a sense of purpose in daily activities, and ensuring that time is spent on what truly matters. This approach enables individuals to make conscious choices about how they invest their time and energy.

The Benefits of Planning with Perspective

Implementing planning with perspective can bring numerous benefits. It helps individuals avoid burnout by identifying periods of rest and rejuvenation. It also enhances decision-making abilities by considering both short-term and long-term consequences. Moreover, it fosters a sense of satisfaction and fulfillment as individuals see progress towards their desired outcomes.

2.5 The Role of Self-Reflection

Self-reflection plays a crucial role in planning with perspective. It involves introspection and self-assessment to gain insight into one's values, strengths, weaknesses, and aspirations. By understanding oneself better, individuals can align their time strategies with their core values and purpose, resulting in a more meaningful and fulfilling life.

Developing a Time Perspective

Building an effective time perspective requires individuals to set clear goals, both short-term and long-term. By breaking down larger goals into smaller, manageable tasks, individuals can create a roadmap for achieving their objectives. Additionally, developing the ability to prioritize tasks based on their importance and urgency allows for better time allocation.

2.7 Balancing Time Allocation

Properly balancing time allocation is crucial to planning with perspective. It involves identifying essential activities, such as work, personal relationships, self-care, and leisure, and allocating an appropriate amount of time to each. Maintaining balance ensures a well-rounded and fulfilling life, preventing burnout and fostering overall well-being.

2.8 Overcoming Obstacles and Distractions

Planning with perspective acknowledges the presence of obstacles and distractions that can hinder effective time management. By recognizing and actively addressing these challenges, individuals can develop strategies to overcome them. Techniques such as setting boundaries, practicing mindfulness, and utilizing technology wisely can help individuals stay focused and maintain productivity.

2.9 Conclusion

This chapter provided an introduction to planning with perspective, emphasizing the significance of effective time management in today's world. By adopting a perspective-oriented approach, individuals can align their time strategies with their values and goals, leading to a more purposeful and fulfilled life. The subsequent chapters will delve deeper into specific techniques and tools that can be employed to build effective time strategies.

CHAPTER 5

Loving and Respecting Others Overview

Spending quality time with your loved ones merely expresses your affection for them. One factor that is seen to be crucial in partnerships is time.

Even with your hectic daily schedule, spending a little time with them can show them how much you value your relationship and make them feel loved. This just implies that spending quality time enables the creation of high-quality reports.

The Greatest Way to Treat People with Love and Respect

Maintaining meaningful personal relationships requires you to treat others with love and respect. You should gain from learning to respect other people's abilities, peculiarities, viewpoints, and efforts because doing so will maintain your interpersonal relationships successful and fulfilling.

By treating oneself with dignity, you may also help yourself advance with confidence, establishing a respectful pattern that you can spread to those around you.

When you respect someone, you are also expressing your affection for them. Respect for someone makes you pay closer attention to what they have to say.

As you may already be aware, your first social skill is to be proactive listening. You enjoy those who listen to you, therefore you should be aware of this. Therefore, once you listen to them, you can safely assume that others adore it as well.

Another method to treat people with respect is to be considerate. Now that you have heard, it is time to respond appropriately. Use the information provided by the other person's body language and voice tone to your advantage when attempting to communicate with them.

Another approach to show people how much you appreciate them is to follow through on your promises. Maintaining your word to someone not only shows them that you are a person of integrity, but it also gives them the impression that you genuinely regard them.

Respecting other people also involves spending a lot of time together. Respecting them must accompany punctuality. You simply show someone you appreciate them when you value their time. Being on time is important, and treating people with respect will hopefully earn you their respect as well.

Be a decent person. Naturally, you will treat someone with the respect you believe they are due. Never cut someone off in a conversation. Remember to be courteous and use the words "please" and "thank you." When you treat someone well, you should make him feel important.

Since love and respect go hand in hand, if you truly love someone, you will treat them with the decency and time they deserve.

Techniques for Effective Time Management

Pomodoro Technique

The Pomodoro Technique is a time management method developed by Francesco Cirillo in the late 1980s. It is designed to enhance productivity and focus by breaking work into intervals, typically 25 minutes in length, followed by short breaks. The technique is named after the tomato-shaped kitchen timer that Cirillo used during his university days, which he called "Pomodoro" (the Italian word for tomato).

The Pomodoro Technique involves the following steps:

Choose a Task: Select a specific task or project that you want to work on.

Set the Timer: Set a timer for 25 minutes (one Pomodoro) and begin working on the chosen task.

Work Intensely: During the Pomodoro interval, focus solely on the task at hand and avoid any distractions or interruptions.

Take a Short Break: When the timer goes off, take a short break of 5 minutes. Use this time to relax, stretch, or do something unrelated to work.

Repeat the Process: After the short break, start another Pomodoro session, continuing to work on the same task. Repeat this cycle until you have completed four Pomodoros.

Take a Longer Break: After completing four Pomodoros (a total of about 2 hours of focused work), take a more extended break of 15-30 minutes. Use this time to recharge and refresh your mind.

Continue the Cycle: Resume the Pomodoro cycle, starting with another 25-minute work interval followed by short breaks and longer breaks as needed.

The Pomodoro Technique is based on the idea that short, focused bursts of work can improve concentration and prevent burnout. The frequent breaks help maintain motivation and prevent mental fatigue. The structured nature of the technique also helps individuals stay accountable and avoid procrastination.

Benefits of the Pomodoro Technique include:

Improved Focus: The time-boxed intervals encourage individuals to stay concentrated on one task at a time, minimizing distractions and increasing focus.

Enhanced Productivity: The technique helps individuals stay productive by breaking work into manageable segments and providing regular breaks for recharging.

Time Awareness: The Pomodoro Technique promotes awareness of how time is used, making it easier to track progress and manage time effectively.

Reduced Procrastination: The structured nature of the technique helps individuals overcome procrastination by breaking tasks into smaller, less intimidating parts.

Minimized Overwhelm: Breaking work into short intervals and manageable chunks makes complex tasks feel more achievable and less overwhelming.

Increased Accountability: The use of timers and intervals keeps individuals accountable for the time they spend on tasks.

Flexibility: The Pomodoro Technique can be adapted to different preferences and work styles, making it suitable for various individuals.

The Pomodoro Technique has gained popularity and is widely used by students, professionals, and anyone seeking a structured approach to time management and improved productivity.

Overview of the technique and its benefits

The **Pomodoro Technique** is a popular time management method that helps individuals improve focus, productivity, and time awareness. It was developed by Francesco Cirillo in the late 1980s and is named after the tomato-shaped kitchen timer he used during university, called "Pomodoro" (the Italian word for tomato). The technique is based on the idea of breaking work into short intervals, usually 25 minutes, called "Pomodoros," followed by short breaks.

Overview of the Pomodoro Technique and its benefits:

How It Works:

Choose a task: Select a specific task or project you want to work on.

Set a timer: Set a timer for 25 minutes and start working on the chosen task with full focus.

Work intensely: During the Pomodoro interval, work on the task without any distractions or interruptions.

Take a short break: When the timer goes off, take a 5-minute break to relax and recharge.

Repeat and track progress: After the short break, start another Pomodoro session, continuing to work on the same task. After completing four

Pomodoros, take a longer break of 15-30 minutes. Then, resume the cycle.

Benefits of the Pomodoro Technique:

Improved focus: By working in short, focused intervals, individuals can concentrate better and maintain attention on the task at hand.

Enhanced productivity: The structured nature of the technique helps individuals stay on track and accomplish more in less time.

Time awareness: The Pomodoro Technique encourages individuals to be more aware of how they spend their time, leading to better time management.

Reduced procrastination: Breaking work into manageable intervals makes tasks feel less overwhelming and helps overcome procrastination.

Minimized burnout: Regular short breaks prevent mental fatigue and burnout, promoting a healthier work pace.

Accountability: The technique uses timers and intervals to hold individuals accountable for their work time.

Flexibility: The Pomodoro Technique can be adapted to different work styles and preferences, making it suitable for a wide range of individuals.

Tips for Using the Pomodoro Technique:

Choose tasks wisely: Prioritize tasks that require focus and avoid using the technique for tasks that can be completed quickly.

Set realistic goals: Be realistic about the number of Pomodoros needed for a task and adjust as necessary.

Eliminate distractions: During the Pomodoro intervals, eliminate distractions such as social media and notifications.

Adapt intervals as needed: Adjust the length of Pomodoro intervals and breaks to suit individual preferences and energy levels.

In conclusion, the Pomodoro Technique is a valuable time management tool that promotes focused work, increased productivity, and better time awareness. By breaking tasks into manageable intervals and taking regular breaks, individuals can maintain their motivation and achieve their goals with more efficiency and effectiveness.

Steps to implement the Pomodoro Technique effectively

Implementing the Pomodoro Technique effectively involves establishing a structured routine and maintaining discipline. Here are the steps to implement the Pomodoro Technique successfully:

Understand the Technique: Familiarize yourself with the concept and principles of the Pomodoro Technique. Understand how the intervals and breaks work to maximize your productivity.

Set Clear Goals: Identify the tasks or projects you want to work on using the Pomodoro Technique. Define clear goals for each session to maintain focus and motivation.

Gather the Required Tools: Gather a timer (or use a Pomodoro app), pen, and paper or a task list to keep track of your Pomodoro sessions and breaks.

Set the Timer: Start a Pomodoro timer for 25 minutes. During this time, focus solely on the task at hand, avoiding distractions and interruptions.

Work Intensely: Work diligently during the Pomodoro interval without switching to other tasks. If any unrelated thoughts come to mind, jot them down and continue working.

Take Short Breaks: When the timer goes off, take a 5-minute break. Use this time to relax, stretch, or do something unrelated to work to recharge your energy.

Repeat the Cycle: After the short break, start another Pomodoro session, continuing to work on the same task. Aim to complete four Pomodoros (2 hours of focused work) before taking a more extended break.

Track Progress: Keep track of completed Pomodoro sessions and breaks using a task list or Pomodoro app. This tracking helps you stay accountable and motivates you to keep going.

Adjust Intervals as Needed: Adapt the length of Pomodoro intervals and breaks based on your energy levels and the nature of the task. Some people may prefer shorter or longer intervals.

Eliminate Distractions: During Pomodoro sessions, eliminate distractions such as social media, notifications, and unrelated tasks. Create a focused work environment.

Plan Longer Breaks: After completing four Pomodoros, take a more extended break of 15-30 minutes. Use this time to relax, refresh, and clear your mind before resuming work.

Be Flexible: While the Pomodoro Technique provides a structured approach, be flexible when necessary. Adjust the schedule to accommodate unexpected events or changes in priorities.

Celebrate Accomplishments: Celebrate your achievements and progress after completing each Pomodoro or task. Acknowledge your efforts to stay motivated.

Practice Regularly: Consistency is key to making the Pomodoro Technique a habit. Practice regularly to improve your focus and productivity over time.

By following these steps and committing to the Pomodoro Technique, you can enhance your productivity, maintain focus, and achieve your goals with more efficiency and effectiveness.

B. Eisenhower Matrix

Understanding the importance and urgency matrix

Important and Urgent - Do First

These are tasks that have both high importance and high urgency. They require immediate attention and must be dealt with promptly. Examples include pressing deadlines, emergencies, and critical issues.

Quadrant 2: Important but Not Urgent - Schedule

These tasks are important but don't require immediate attention. They contribute to long-term goals, personal growth, and strategic planning.

tasks should be scheduled and planned for completion. Examples include goal setting, long-term projects, and relationship-building activities.

Urgent but Not Important - Delegate

Tasks in this quadrant are urgent but do not contribute significantly to long-term goals or priorities. They often involve interruptions, distractions, and activities that can be handled by others. These tasks should be delegated whenever possible to free up time for more important work.

Not Important and Not Urgent - Don't Do

These tasks have low importance and low urgency. They are time-wasters and distractions that do not contribute to personal or organizational goals. Quadrant 4 tasks should be minimized or eliminated to avoid wasting time and resources.

Understanding the Importance and Urgency Matrix:

Prioritization: The Eisenhower Matrix provides a clear framework for prioritizing tasks. It helps individuals identify what needs immediate attention (Quadrant 1) and what can be scheduled or delegated (Quadrants 2 and 3) to focus on the most critical activities.

Time Management: The matrix encourages individuals to spend more time in Quadrant 2, focusing on important but not urgent tasks that contribute to long-term success. By planning and scheduling these tasks, individuals can avoid constant firefighting and reduce stress.

Proactivity: Emphasizing Quadrant 2 activities promotes a proactive approach to work and life.

By focusing on prevention and preparation, individuals can reduce the number of tasks that fall into the urgent and important category .

Elimination of Time-Wasters: Quadrant 4 tasks are often time-wasters that can be eliminated from daily routines. By being aware of these distractions, individuals can reclaim valuable time for more meaningful activities.

Delegation: The matrix encourages individuals to delegate tasks that are urgent but not important . Delegating these tasks to others empowers the team and frees up time for higher-priority work.

By using the Eisenhower Matrix, individuals can make better decisions about how to allocate their time and energy, leading to improved time management, increased productivity, and better alignment with long-term goals.

Applying the Eisenhower Matrix to prioritize tasks

Avoiding Procrastination

Applying the Eisenhower Matrix to prioritize tasks is an effective way to overcome procrastination and stay focused on what truly matters. Here's how you can use the matrix to prioritize tasks and avoid procrastination:

List Your Tasks: Begin by listing all the tasks you need to complete. This could be a mix of work-related tasks, personal responsibilities, and other to-dos.

Evaluate Importance: Assess the importance of each task. Consider how each task aligns with your goals, values, and long-term objectives. Tasks that directly contribute to your success or well-being should be categorized as "Important."

Assess Urgency: Determine the urgency of each task. Identify deadlines and time-sensitive activities that require immediate attention. Tasks with imminent deadlines or consequences should be labeled as "Urgent."

Apply the Matrix: Place each task into one of the four quadrants based on its importance and urgency:

- Quadrant 1 (Important and Urgent): These tasks require immediate action and should be tackled first. Prioritize them based on their impact and deadline.

- Quadrant 2 (Important but Not Urgent): These tasks are crucial for your long-term success and well-being. Schedule dedicated time for them to avoid last-minute rushes.

- Quadrant 3 (Urgent but Not Important): These tasks may seem urgent, but they don't contribute significantly to your goals. Whenever possible, delegate or minimize the time spent on them.

Quadrant 4:; These tasks are time-wasters and distractions. Avoid them as much as possible to prevent procrastination.

Focus on Quadrant 1 and 2: Once you have prioritized your tasks, concentrate on completing tasks in Quadrant 1 and Quadrant 2 first. These tasks are the most meaningful and will have the greatest impact on your success and well-being.

Delegate or Eliminate Quadrant 3 and 4 Tasks: Be proactive in delegating or eliminating tasks in Quadrant 3 and By avoiding time-wasting activities and sharing the workload, you free up more time to focus on important and urgent tasks.

Set Specific Goals: Set clear goals and deadlines for the tasks in Quadrant By having specific objectives, you create a sense of purpose and urgency for these important tasks, reducing the likelihood of procrastination.

Use Time Management Techniques: Combine the Eisenhower Matrix with other time management techniques, such as the Pomodoro Technique, to enhance your focus and productivity.

Review and Adjust: Regularly review and update your task list and the placement of tasks in the Eisenhower Matrix. As priorities change or new tasks arise, adjust your approach accordingly.

Celebrate Achievements: Celebrate your accomplishments, no matter how small. Recognizing your progress and successes can boost motivation and combat procrastination.

By consistently applying the Eisenhower Matrix to prioritize tasks, you can overcome procrastination, make better use of your time, and achieve your goals with greater efficiency and focus.

Identifying common causes of procrastination

Procrastination is a common behavior where individuals delay or avoid tasks that need to be done. It can be a significant obstacle to productivity and goal achievement. Identifying the common causes of procrastination can help individuals address the root issues and develop strategies to overcome it. Here are some common causes of procrastination:

Lack of Clarity: Unclear goals or tasks can lead to procrastination. When individuals are unsure about what needs to be done or how to approach a task, they may put it off.

Fear of Failure: Fear of failure can paralyze individuals, making them hesitant to start or complete a task. Procrastination can be a way to avoid facing the possibility of not meeting expectations.

Perfectionism: A desire for perfection can lead to procrastination because individuals may delay starting a task until they believe they can execute it flawlessly.

Overwhelm: Feeling overwhelmed by a large or complex task can lead to avoidance and procrastination. Breaking the task into smaller, manageable steps can help overcome this.

Lack of Motivation: A lack of interest or motivation in a task can cause procrastination. When individuals don't see the value or relevance of a task, they may postpone it.

Distractions: Easily accessible distractions, such as social media, entertainment, or constant notifications, can divert individuals' attention from their tasks, leading to procrastination.

Poor Time Management: Inadequate time management skills can cause individuals to underestimate the time needed for a task, resulting in delays and procrastination.

Low Energy Levels: Fatigue or low energy levels can reduce productivity and lead to procrastination. Feeling physically or mentally drained can make starting a task more challenging.

Lack of Accountability: When there are no external consequences or accountability for completing a task, individuals may postpone it.

Task Aversion: Certain tasks may be unpleasant or boring, leading to task aversion and procrastination.

1 Decision Paralysis: Having too many choices or options can create decision paralysis, making it difficult to start a task.

1 Lack of Prioritization: When tasks are not properly prioritized, individuals may spend time

on less important tasks while avoiding critical ones.

1 Underestimating the Task Difficulty: If a task is perceived as too difficult or beyond one's capabilities, procrastination can occur as a coping mechanism.

1 Fear of Success: Surprisingly, fear of success can also lead to procrastination. Individuals may fear the changes and responsibilities that success may bring.

1 Lack of Rewards: When individuals don't see immediate or meaningful rewards for completing a task, they may delay working on it.

Understanding the underlying causes of procrastination can help individuals develop strategies to overcome it. By addressing these root issues, individuals can foster better time management, improve motivation, and cultivate a proactive approach to their tasks.

Strategies to overcome procrastination and stay focused

Overcoming procrastination and staying focused requires a combination of self-awareness, discipline, and effective time management techniques. Here are some strategies to help you conquer procrastination and maintain focus:

Set Clear Goals: Define specific, achievable, and time-bound goals. Knowing what you want to accomplish provides motivation and direction, making it easier to stay focused.

Break Tasks into Smaller Steps: Divide large or overwhelming tasks into smaller, more manageable steps. Tackling one step at a time makes the task feel less daunting and helps maintain progress.

Use the Pomodoro Technique: Work in focused intervals (e.g., 25 minutes) followed by short breaks. The Pomodoro Technique helps maintain concentration and prevents burnout.

Prioritize Tasks: Use the Eisenhower Matrix to prioritize tasks based on importance and urgency. Focus on the most important and urgent tasks first.

Set Deadlines: Assign specific deadlines to tasks and hold yourself accountable for meeting them. Deadlines create a sense of urgency and prevent procrastination.

Minimize Distractions: Identify and eliminate or minimize distractions in your environment. Create a dedicated workspace and silence unnecessary notifications.

Establish a Routine: Develop a daily or weekly routine that includes dedicated time for important tasks. Consistent routines build habits and reduce the likelihood of procrastination.

Reward Yourself: Set up a reward system for completing tasks. Treat yourself to something enjoyable after completing a challenging task as positive reinforcement.

Visualize Success: Imagine the satisfaction and benefits of completing the task. Visualizing success can boost motivation and reduce procrastination.

Use Positive Self-talk: Replace negative thoughts and self-doubt with positive affirmations. Encourage yourself and remind yourself of your capabilities.

1 Minimize Perfectionism: Strive for excellence, but avoid perfectionism. Accept that tasks may not always be flawless and focus on progress rather than perfection.

1 Seek Accountability: Share your goals with a friend, family member, or colleague who can hold

you accountable. Regular check-ins can help you stay on track.

1 Practice Mindfulness: Stay present and focused on the task at hand. Mindfulness can reduce distractions and improve concentration.

1 Remove Decision Fatigue: Make important decisions in advance, so you don't waste time on trivial choices during the day.

1 Get Started: Often, the most challenging part is getting started. Commit to working on a task for just a few minutes, and once you start, momentum will build.

1 Review Progress Regularly: Reflect on your progress and accomplishments regularly. Celebrate successes and adjust your approach as needed.

1 Seek Support: If you consistently struggle with procrastination, consider seeking support from a

coach, therapist, or counselor to address underlying issues.

Remember that overcoming procrastination is an ongoing process that requires patience and persistence. Experiment with different strategies to find what works best for you, and don't be too hard on yourself if you slip up occasionally. With determination and effort, you can develop the habits and mindset needed to conquer procrastination and maintain focus on your goals.

CHAPTER 6

Assessing Your Current Time Usage

1. Time Tracking: Keep a record of how you spend each hour throughout the day. This provides insights into patterns, revealing where time is invested productively and where it might be wasted.

2. Identifying Time Drains: Recognize activities that consume more time than necessary or those that offer minimal value. These time drains can range from excessive social media use to prolonged periods of indecision.

3. Analysis of Prioritization: Evaluate whether you are allocating time in alignment with your priorities. Assess if essential tasks are receiving the attention they deserve or if less critical activities are taking precedence.

4. Reflection on Productivity: Consider your energy levels and focus during different times of the day. Determine when you are most productive and strategize to tackle high-priority tasks during these peak periods.

5. Goal Alignment: Connect your daily activities with overarching goals. Assess whether your current time usage contributes effectively to your short-term and long-term objectives.

6. Feedback from Others: Seek input from colleagues, friends, or family members. External perspectives can provide valuable insights into time management blind spots or areas for improvement.

1. Recording Activities: Keep a detailed log of your activities throughout the day. Note the start and end times of each task, including work-related responsibilities, personal activities, breaks, and leisure.

2. Categorizing Tasks: Organize recorded activities into categories such as work, leisure, family, personal development, and chores. This categorization helps identify the primary areas where your time is invested.

3. Assessing Time Intensity: Assign time intensity levels to each activity. Determine whether tasks are high, medium, or low in terms of time commitment and energy expenditure.

4. Identifying Time Drains: Analyze the recorded data to pinpoint activities that consume more time than necessary or contribute less value. Identify habits or distractions that may be potential time drains.

5. Evaluating Prioritization: Reflect on whether your time allocation aligns with your priorities. Assess if crucial tasks are receiving sufficient attention or if less significant activities are taking up a disproportionate amount of time.

6. Reviewing Patterns: Look for patterns in your daily routine. Identify peak productivity periods and times when focus tends to wane. This awareness can guide you in scheduling tasks at optimal times.

7. Setting Goals for Improvement: Based on the audit findings, establish goals for more efficient time management. This might include reducing time spent on non-essential activities, optimizing daily routines, or allocating more time to high-priority tasks.

8. Conducting a personal time audit is a proactive step toward understanding your time utilization. It provides a foundation for informed decision-making, helping you make adjustments to optimize your schedule and achieve a better balance between productivity and personal well-being.

1. Analysis of Daily Activities: Review your daily schedule and activities to identify tasks that consistently take longer than expected or contribute less value to your goals.

2. Distractions and Interruptions: Recognize common distractions and interruptions that disrupt your workflow. These can include frequent social media checks, excessive emails, or interruptions from colleagues.

3. Procrastination Patterns: Identify areas where procrastination tends to occur. Understanding the reasons behind procrastination helps in developing strategies to overcome this time-draining habit.

4. Inefficient Processes: Evaluate your work processes to identify any inefficiencies. This could involve redundant steps, lack of organization, or using outdated tools and methods.

5. Unproductive Meetings: Assess the necessity and effectiveness of meetings. Unproductive or overly lengthy meetings can be significant time drains. Consider alternatives such as concise updates or utilizing collaborative tools.

6. Undefined Goals: Lack of clear goals and priorities can lead to scattered efforts and wasted time. Ensure that you have well-defined objectives, allowing you to allocate time purposefully.

7. Overcommitting: Recognize instances where you may be overcommitting to tasks or projects. Setting realistic expectations prevents overextension and potential burnout.

8. Failure to Delegate: Evaluate whether you are shouldering too much responsibility. Delegating tasks to others, when appropriate, can free up valuable time for more strategic and high-impact activities.

1. Gradual Progress: Realistic expectations acknowledge that change is often a gradual process. It's essential to understand that transforming habits and routines takes time and consistent effort.

2. Avoiding Overwhelm: Ambitious goals are commendable, but they should be balanced with practicality. Setting realistic expectations prevents the feeling of overwhelm that can arise when trying to make too many changes at once.

3. Sustainable Change: Realistic expectations contribute to sustainable change. Rather than pursuing quick fixes, focus on developing habits and practices that can be maintained in the long term.

4. Adaptability: Life is dynamic, and circumstances change. Realistic expectations allow for adaptability, recognizing that adjustments may be

necessary based on evolving priorities and situations.

5. Celebrating Small Wins: Acknowledge and celebrate small victories along the way. Realistic expectations highlight the significance of incremental progress, reinforcing positive behaviors and fostering motivation.

6. Learning from Setbacks: Realistic expectations also recognize that setbacks are a natural part of the change process. Use setbacks as learning opportunities, adjusting strategies as needed without losing sight of the overall goal.

7. Balancing Ambition and Realism: While it's essential to aspire to significant improvements, setting expectations that balance ambition with realism ensures a more sustainable and positive journey toward change.

Chapter 7

Creating Your Personalized Time Management System

Creating a personalized time management system begins with assessing your current style and habits. Understanding how you currently manage time lays the foundation for developing a system that suits your needs and preferences. Here's a step-by-step guide:

Self-Assessment:

1. Time Audit: Start by tracking how you spend your time for a week or two. Note activities, their duration, and their significance. Use apps or journals to record this data.

2. Identify Patterns: Look for recurring themes. Are there specific times of the day when you're most productive? Are there consistent distractions or time sinks?

3. Assess Effectiveness: Evaluate the outcomes of your tasks. Are you completing high-priority tasks on time? Are there tasks taking longer than expected?

4. Emotional Assessment: Reflect on how certain tasks make you feel. Do you procrastinate on certain tasks? Are there activities that drain your energy?

Understanding Your Style:

1. Work Preferences: Determine if you thrive with structured schedules or prefer flexibility. Are you a morning person or more productive during specific times?

2. Task Handling: Analyze if you prefer tackling smaller tasks first or diving into larger, more challenging projects immediately.

3. Distraction Management: Identify common distractions and understand how you deal with

them. Do you easily get sidetracked by emails, social media, or interruptions?

4. Stress Assessment: Evaluate stress triggers related to time management. Are you often overwhelmed by deadlines or juggling multiple tasks?

Designing Your System:

1. Set Clear Goals: Define short-term and long-term goals. Break them down into actionable steps with deadlines.

2. Choose Techniques: Select time management techniques that resonate with your style. Whether it's time blocking, Pomodoro, or another method, experiment to find what suits you.

3. Plan Your Schedule: Structure your day according to your energy levels and preferences. Allocate time blocks for specific tasks or categories of work.

4. Implement Changes Gradually: Don't overhaul your routine entirely. Start with small adjustments based on your assessment and gradually incorporate changes.

5. Regular Review: Continuously evaluate the effectiveness of your system. Adjust as needed based on evolving priorities and experiences.

Creating a personalized time management system is an ongoing process. It's about understanding yourself, your habits, and your objectives. By tailoring time management techniques to suit your individual style, you'll craft a system that optimizes productivity and supports your overall well-being.

Designing a custom time management system tailored to your lifestyle and goals involves a personalized approach. Here's a step-by-step guide to crafting a system that aligns with your unique needs:

Define Your Goals and Priorities:

Clarify Objectives: Outline both short-term and long-term goals. Define what success means for you in various aspects of life: career, personal development, relationships, health, etc.

Prioritize Tasks: Identify tasks aligned with your goals. Categorize them based on urgency, importance, and impact.

Assess Your Lifestyle and Preferences:

Work Style: Understand your peak productivity hours. Determine if you prefer a structured routine or need flexibility.

Energy Levels: Recognize when you feel most energized and productive during the day.

Distractions and Habits: Identify common distractions and habits that affect your productivity negatively.

Designing the System:

Choose Time Management Techniques: Based on your assessment, select techniques that resonate with your preferences. It could be time blocking, batching similar tasks, or setting specific daily priorities.

Create a Structured Schedule: Design a daily or weekly schedule that integrates your peak productivity hours with allocated time blocks for different tasks or activities.

Utilize Tools and Technology: Incorporate tools or apps that complement your system, aiding in task management, reminders, or time tracking, aligning with your preferences.

Experiment and Adjust: Start implementing your system gradually. Experiment with different approaches and be open to adjusting based on what works best for you.

Implementation and Review:

Consistency and Adaptability: Commit to following your designed system consistently. Stay adaptable and open to fine-tuning based on experiences and changes in goals or lifestyle.

Regular Evaluation: Schedule periodic reviews to assess the effectiveness of your system. Adjustments might be necessary to ensure alignment with your evolving goals and preferences.

Self-compassion: Acknowledge that adapting to a new system takes time. Be patient with yourself through the learning process.

Key Considerations:

- Flexibility: Allow room for unexpected events or changes in priorities within your system.

- Self-Care: Incorporate breaks, relaxation, and activities that rejuvenate you into your schedule.

- Mindfulness: Stay mindful of how you spend your time and ensure alignment with your goals.

Customizing a time management system that fits your lifestyle and goals involves trial and error. Embrace the process of discovery and adaptation, aiming to create a system that optimizes productivity while nurturing a balanced and fulfilling life.

- Tips for prioritizing tasks and setting realistic goals

Prioritizing tasks and setting realistic goals are essential skills for effective time management. Here are some tips to help with both:

Prioritizing Tasks:

1. Eisenhower Matrix: Use this matrix to categorize tasks into four quadrants based on

urgency and importance. Focus on tasks that are both urgent and important first.

2. ABCD Method: Prioritize tasks by labeling them A (high priority), B (medium priority), C (low priority), and D (delegate). This helps in focusing on crucial tasks.

3. Time-Sensitive Tasks: Identify tasks with set deadlines and prioritize them accordingly to avoid last-minute rushes.

4. Consider Impact: Evaluate tasks based on their potential impact. Some tasks might not be urgent but could have significant long-term benefits.

5. Focus on Your Strengths: Prioritize tasks aligned with your strengths and expertise, allowing for more efficient completion.

Setting Realistic Goals:

1. Specific and Measurable: Define clear, specific goals that are measurable. Instead of "improve

sales," aim for "increase sales by 15% in six months."

2. Break Down Goals: Divide larger goals into smaller, manageable milestones. This makes them less overwhelming and easier to track progress.

3. SMART Criteria: Ensure goals are Specific, Measurable, Achievable, Relevant, and Time-bound. This framework helps in setting clear and achievable objectives.

4. Consider Resources: Evaluate the resources required to achieve your goals—time, finances, skills, etc. Set goals that are feasible within your available resources.

5. Review and Adjust: Regularly review your goals. If needed, adjust them based on changing circumstances or new information without compromising the overall vision.

CHAPTER 8

UNDERSTANDING PRIORITIZATION TECHNIQUES

The secret to good time management amid the maze of everyday activities and obligations rests not just in how much you can do but, more significantly, in what you choose to accomplish. Prioritization is the crux that separates simple activity from actual productivity. In this chapter, we will look at three strong tools—the Eisenhower Matrix, the ABCD Method, and the Pareto Principle—that can help you make informed decisions about where to focus your time and energy.

Urgent vs. Important in the Eisenhower Matrix

This matrix, named after President Dwight D. Eisenhower, is a basic yet effective tool for classifying activities depending on their urgency and relevance. The Eisenhower Matrix divides your tasks into four quadrants and challenges you to analyze the relevance of each action, steering your emphasis toward tasks that actually correspond with your goals.

Quadrant I: Urgency and Priority (Do First)

This quadrant's tasks need urgent attention. They are crucial to your objectives and frequently require deadlines. Prioritize and complete these activities as soon as possible to minimize the stress of last-minute rushing.

Critical but Not Urgent

Activities that contribute significantly to your long-term goals but have no immediate deadlines can be found here. Make time for these chores to avoid them becoming urgent and to encourage proactive, strategic planning.

Urgent but Not Critical

Tasks in this quadrant may appear urgent, but they may not fit with your primary goals. Consider delegating or finding effective ways to reduce the amount of time spent on them, allowing you to focus on high-impact tasks.

Quadrant IV: Not Urgent or Important (Remove)

These are time-wasters and diversions that neither contribute to nor demand your immediate attention. Consider removing or reducing these tasks to free up time.

Categorizing Tasks for Priority Using the ABCD Method

The ABCD Method, commonly known as the Eisenhower Box, delves deeper into prioritization by adding another layer of classification within each grid quadrant.

High Priority (Must Do) A-Tasks

Determine which tasks are critical to your goals and achievement. These are non-negotiable and must be addressed immediately.

B-Tasks are of medium priority (should be completed).

These tasks help you achieve your goals but may not be as time-sensitive. After you've completed your A-tasks, make time for them.

Low Priority (Could Do) C-Tasks

Tasks in this category are enjoyable to do but are not vital to your objectives. If higher-priority activities are accomplished, consider dedicating time to them.

Delegate or Eliminate (Don't Do) D-Tasks

Tasks in this category may not be relevant to your objectives or may be better suited to others. When possible, delegate or remove tasks that do not add significantly to your goals.

The Pareto Principle (the 80/20 Rule): Prioritizing High-Impact Tasks

According to the Pareto Principle, around 80% of results come from 20% of efforts. This idea, when applied to time management, implies that a minority of your work will contribute to the majority of your intended outcomes. You may greatly increase your productivity by finding and focusing on these high-impact tasks.

Finding the Critical Few (20%)

Identify projects that are most directly related to your goals and have the potential to provide significant outcomes. These are the "vital few" chores that require your undivided attention.

Reducing the Trivial many (80%)

Recognize that not all tasks contribute equally to your objectives. Reduce or assign less important duties to make room for the critical few.

Remember that flexibility is essential when you incorporate these prioritizing tactics into your everyday practice. Priorities might evolve, and new emergencies can emerge. The idea is not rigid adherence, but rather a fluid and deliberate approach to allocating your time based on the ever-changing landscape of your goals and obligations.

www.ingramcontent.com/pod-product-compliance
Lightning Source LLC
LaVergne TN
LVHW010601070526
838199LV00063BA/5035